01 PRE-SHOOT CHECKLIST

Check these settings before you head out with your camera!

SETTING	MY PREFERRED SETTING
☑ Shooting Mode	....
☑ White Balance Setting	....
☑ ISO Setting	
☑ Focus Mode	
☑ AF-Area Mode	
☑ Release Mode	
☑ Metering Mode	
☑ Bracketing: On/Off	....
☑ File Format: JPEG/HEIF, RAW, or RAW+JPEG/HEIF	....
☑ Highlight Warning: On/Off	....
☑ Vibration Reduction: On/Off/Sport	....
☑ Picture Control	....
☑ Flash Mode	....
☑ Battery Fully Charged and In Camera	....
☑ Memory Card(s) Formatted and In Camera	....

02 BUTTONS, DIALS, AND SCREENS

CAMERA BODY TOP

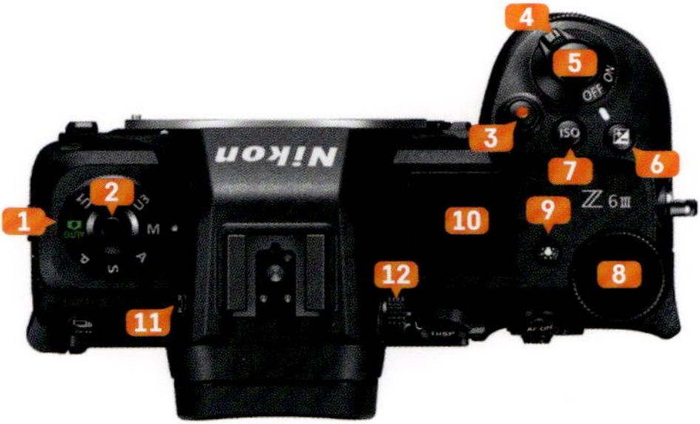

1. **Mode Dial:** Press and rotate the Mode dial to change the Shooting mode between Auto, P (Programmed Auto), A (Aperture Priority), S (Shutter Priority), M (Manual), or User settings 1–3.
2. **Mode Dial Lock Release:** Press to rotate the Mode dial.
3. **Movie Record:** Start and end recording when shooting video.
4. **Power Switch:** Turn camera on and off.
5. **Shutter Release:** Press halfway to activate autofocus and all the way to take the photo.
6. **Exposure Compensation:** Use with the Main Command dial to adjust exposure compensation.

NIKON Z6 III POCKET GUIDE

TABLE OF CONTENTS

7. **ISO:** Press and rotate the Main Command dial to adjust ISO.

8. **Main Command Dial:** Use to adjust camera settings.

9. **Illuminator Button:** Press to illuminate the control panel, press again to turn off.

10. **Control Panel:** Shows multiple camera settings.

11. **Monitor Mode:** Press to cycle between viewfinder and monitor displays.

12. **Diopter Adjustment Control:** Pull out and turn to adjust the diopter in the viewfinder.

CAMERA BODY BACK

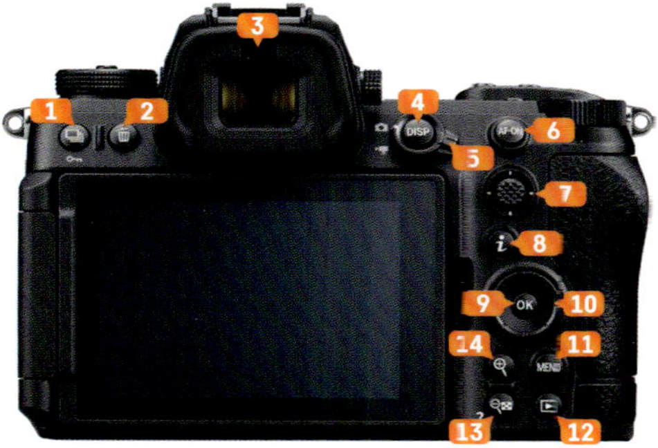

1. **Release/Protect:** Use to set the Release mode/Protect images.
2. **Trash:** Delete current image on LCD.
3. **Eye Sensor:** Switch display from monitor to viewfinder.

4. **DISP:** Cycle through the display screens.
5. **Photo/Movie Selector:** Switch between Photo and Movie modes.
6. **AF-ON:** Press to engage autofocus.
7. **Sub-Selector:** Use as a joystick to select a focus point. Press the center to lock focus and exposure.
8. *i* **Button:** Opens contextual menu, depending on what mode you're in (Movie or Photo).
9. **OK:** Select current option.
10. **Multi Selector:** Navigate menus or select AF point.
11. **MENU:** Opens and closes the menu system.
12. **Playback:** Show last image taken on the LCD.
13. **Zoom Out:** Zoom out on current image shown on the LCD.
14. **Zoom In:** Zoom in on current image shown on the LCD.

CAMERA BODY FRONT

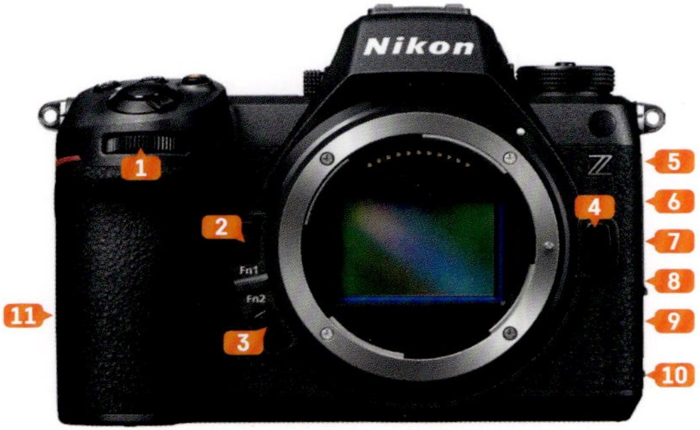

1. **Sub-Command Dial:** Adjust camera settings.
2. **Fn1:** Customizable button. Default is set to White Balance.
3. **Fn2:** Customizable button. Default is set to Focus and AF-Area modes.
4. **Lens Release:** Press button and turn lens to remove it from the camera.
5. **External Microphone/Line In Connector (under cover, right side):** Connect microphone or other audio in to camera.
6. **Headphone Connector (under cover, right side):** Connect headphones to camera.
7. **USB Connector (under cover, right ride):** Connect to USB devices.
8. **HDMI Connector (under cover, right side):** Connect HDMI cable.
9. **Accessory Terminal (under cover, right side):** Connect remote.
10. **Microphone Connector (under cover, right side):** Connect microphone to camera.
11. **Dual Memory Card Slots (under cover, left side):** The top slot takes a CFexpress or XQD memory card, and the bottom slot takes an SD memory card.

CAMERA BODY BOTTOM

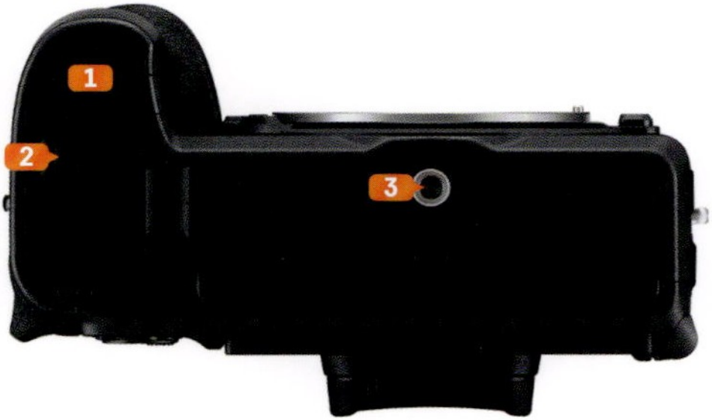

1. **Battery Chamber Cover:** Open to access the camera battery.

2. **Battery Chamber Cover Latch:** Use to open the battery cover. Make sure it is locked after closing the cover.

3. **Tripod Socket:** Standard tripod socket for attaching a tripod or monopod.

VIEWFINDER DISPLAY

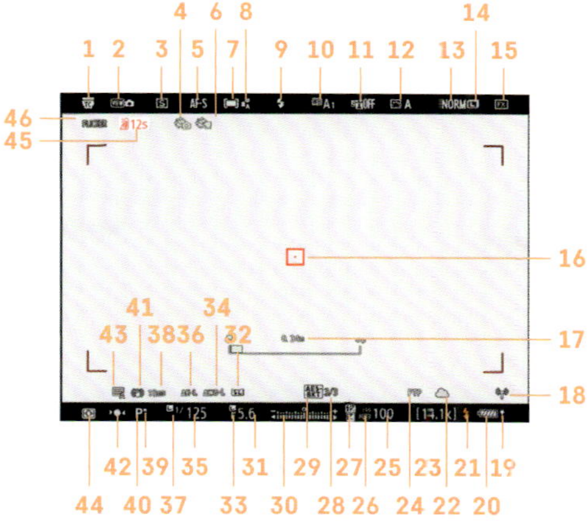

1. Built-In Teleconverter Enabled Icon: Shows when built-in teleconverter is being used.

2. View Mode Icon: Shows when the effects of White Balance, Picture Controls, exposure compensation, and other settings that affect color and exposure are visible in the shooting display.

3. Release Mode: Shows the current Release mode: S (Single Frame), L (Continuous Low), H (Continuous High), H* (Continuous High Extended). [C30] [C60] [C120]: camera takes 30, 60, or 120fps while shutter release is pressed. [Self-Timer] appears when using Self Timer mode.

4. **Interval-Timer Indicator:** Appears when using the interval-timer mode.

5. **Focus Mode:** Shows the current Focus mode: AF-S (Single AF), AF-C (Continuous AF), AF-F (Full-Time AF), MF (Manual Focus).

6. **Time-Lapse Video Indicator:** Shows when camera is in time-lapse shooting mode.

7. **AF-Area Mode:** Shows the current AF-Area mode: Pinpoint, Single-Point AF, Dynamic-Area AF (S, M, L) Wide-Area AF (S, M, C1, C2), 3D-Tracking AF, Subject-Tracking AF, or Auto-Area AF.

8. **Subject Detection Icon:** Shows when and what subject detection is active: Auto, People, Animal, Vehicle, or Airplanes.

9. **Flash Mode:** Shows the current active flash mode.

10. **White Balance:** Shows the current White Balance.

11. **Active D-Lighting:** Shows the status of Active D-Lighting.

12. **Picture Control:** Shows the current Picture Control.

13. **Image Quality:** Shows the current image quality.

14. **Image Size:** Shows the current image size: Large, Medium, or Small.

15. **Image Area:** Shows the current image area.

16. **Focus Point:** Shows the current focus point. Can be positioned by using the Sub-Selector or Multi Selector.

17. **Focus Distance Indicator:** Shows the distance between camera and subject.

18. **Wi-Fi Connection Indicator:** Shows when Wi-Fi is active.

19. **USB Power Delivery:** Shows when the camera is drawing power from a connected USB device.

20. **Battery Indicator:** Displays amount of power left.

21. **Flash Ready Indicator:** Shows when the flash is ready to fire.

22. **Nikon Imaging Cloud:** Connection status.

23. Number of Remaining Exposures: Displays the number of exposures that can be taken based on the memory card's available space.

24. FTP Connection status.

25. ISO: Shows the current ISO.

26. ISO Sensitivity Indicator: Shows if Auto ISO is engaged.

27. Flash Compensation Indicator (top): Shows if flash compensation is being applied. **Exposure Compensation Indicator (bottom):** Shows if exposure compensation is being applied.

28. Number of shots in current set bracketing mode.

29. Exposure and Flash bracketing indicator.

30. Exposure Indicator/Exposure Compensation Display/Auto Bracketing: Shows the current exposure/Shows any exposure compensation being applied/Shows any auto bracketing exposure being applied.

31. Aperture: Shows the current aperture.

32. FV Lock Indicator: Shows when the flash value is locked.

33. Aperture Lock: Shows when aperture lock is applied.

34. Auto White Balance Lock: Shows when active.

35. Shutter Speed: Shows the current shutter speed.

36. Auto Exposure Lock: Shows when active.

37. Shutter Speed Lock Icon: Shows when shutter speed is locked.

38. Focal Length: Shows the current focal length.

39. Flexible Program Indicator: When using P shooting mode, you can rotate the Main Command dial to change the exposure settings without changing the overall exposure. This flexible program adjustment will cause this icon to appear next to the P in the display.

40. Shooting Mode: Shows the current Shooting mode (Auto, P, S, A, M).

41. Vibration Reduction Indicator: Indicates if Vibration Reduction is active (On/Sports); not shown if VR is off.

42. Focus Indicator: Shows when the subject is in focus by turning the middle circle solid.

43. Shutter Type: Shows the type of shutter being used, either the mechanical shutter or the electronic front-curtain shutter. Or set it to Auto, and the camera selects the shutter type.

44. Metering: Shows the current Metering mode.

45. Temperature Warning: Shows when camera is getting overheated.

46. Flicker Detection: Shows when Flicker Detection is active. Helps reduce the effects of flicker from fluorescent and mercury-vapor light.

MONITOR DISPLAY

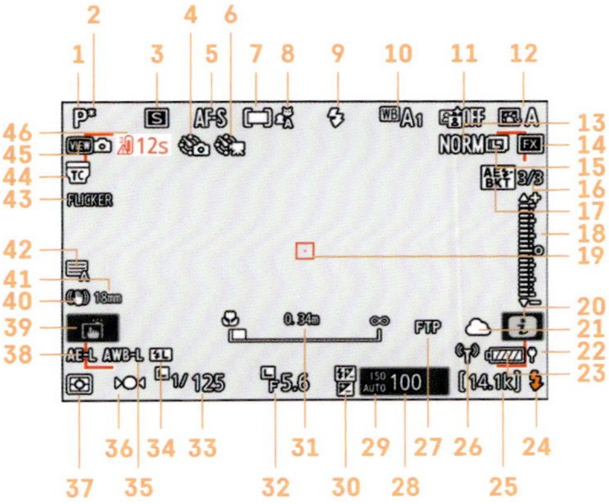

1. **Shooting Mode:** Shows the current Shooting mode (Auto, P, S, A, M).
2. **Flexible Program Indicator:** When using P shooting mode, you can rotate the Main Command dial to change the exposure settings without changing the overall exposure. This flexible program adjustment will cause this icon to appear next to the P in the display.
3. **Release Mode:** Shows the current Release mode: S (Single Frame), L (Continuous Low), H (Continuous High), H* (Continuous High Extended). [C30] [C60] [C120]: camera takes 30, 60, or 120fps while shutter release is pressed. [Self-Timer] when in Self Timer mode.
4. **Interval-Timer Indicator:** Appears when using the interval-timer mode.
5. **Focus Mode:** Shows the current Focus mode: AF-S (Single AF), AF-C (Continuous AF), AF-F (Full-Time AF), MF (Manual Focus).
6. **Time-Lapse Video Indicator:** Shows when the camera is in time-lapse shooting mode.
7. **AF-Area Mode:** Shows the current AF-Area mode: Pinpoint, Single-Point AF, Dynamic-Area AF (S, M, L), Wide-Area AF (S, M, C1, C2), 3D-Tracking AF, Subject-Tracking AF, or Auto-Area AF.
8. **Subject Detection Icon:** Shows when and what subject detection is active: Auto, People, Animal, Vehicle, or Airplanes.
9. **Flash Mode:** Shows the current active flash mode.
10. **White Balance:** Shows the current White Balance.
11. **Active D-Lighting:** Shows the status of Active D-Lighting.
12. **Picture Control:** Shows the current Picture Control.
13. **Image Quality:** Shows the current image quality.
14. **Image Area:** Shows the current image area.
15. **Image Size:** Shows the current image size: Large, Medium, or Small.

16. **Number of shots in current set bracketing mode.**

17. **Exposure and Flash bracketing indicator.**

18. **Exposure Indicator/Exposure Compensation Display/Auto Bracketing:** Shows the current exposure/Shows any exposure compensation being applied/Shows any auto bracketing exposure being applied.

19. **Focus Point:** Shows the current focus point. Can be positioned by using the Sub-Selector or Multi Selector.

20. ***i* Icon:** Use for quick access to frequently used settings.

21. **Nikon Imaging Cloud:** Connection status.

22. **USB Power Delivery:** Shows when the camera is drawing power from a connected USB device.

23. **Battery Indicator:** Displays amount of power left.

24. **Flash Ready Indicator:** Shows when the flash is ready to fire.

25. **Number of Remaining Exposures:** Displays the number of exposures that can be taken based on the memory card's available space.

26. **Wi-Fi Connection Indicator:** Shows when Wi-Fi is active.

27. **FTP Connection status.**

28. **ISO:** Shows the current ISO.

29. **ISO Sensitivity Indicator:** Shows if Auto ISO is engaged.

30. **Flash Compensation Indicator (top):** Shows if flash compensation is being applied. **Exposure Compensation Indicator (bottom):** Shows if exposure compensation is being applied.

31. **Focus Distance Indicator:** Shows the distance between camera and subject.

32. **Aperture:** Shows the current aperture.

33. **Shutter Speed:** Shows the current shutter speed.

34. **FV Lock Indicator:** Shows when the flash value is locked.

35. **Auto White Balance Lock:** Shows when active.

36. **Focus Indicator:** Shows when the subject is in focus by turning the middle circle solid.

37. **Metering:** Shows the current Metering mode.

38. **Auto Exposure Lock:** Shows when active.

39. **Touch Shooting:** Shows when active.

40. **Vibration Reduction Indicator:** Indicates if Vibration Reduction is active (On/Sports), not shown if VR is off.

41. **Focal Length:** Shows current focal length.

42. **Shutter Type:** Shows the type of shutter being used, either the mechanical shutter or the electronic front-curtain shutter. Or set it to Auto, and the camera selects the shutter type.

43. **Flicker Detection:** Shows when Flicker Detection is active. Helps reduce the effects of flicker from fluorescent and mercury-vapor light.

44. **Built-In Teleconverter Enabled Icon:** Shows when built-in teleconverter is being used.

45. **Live View Preview Indicator:** Shows the effects of the current White Balance, Picture Controls, and Exposure Compensation settings on the image before the photo is taken.

46. **Temperature Warning:** Shows when camera is getting overheated.

VIEWFINDER DISPLAY (MOVIE)

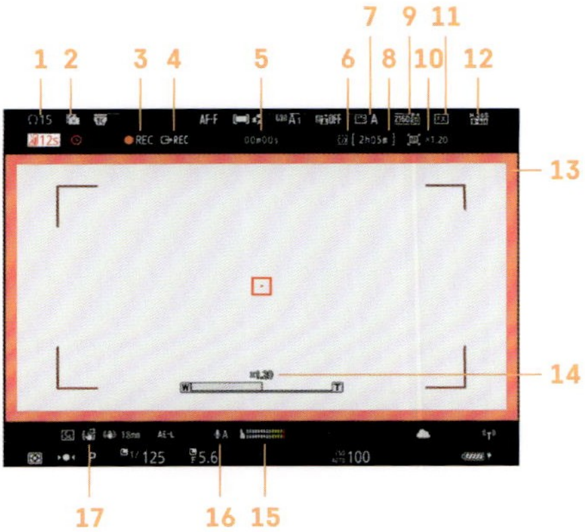

1. Headphone Volume: Shows the current headphone volume. Use the up and down keys on the Multi Selector to adjust the volume.

2. Zebra Pattern: When active, it shows if a zebra pattern is being used to show tone range.

3. Recording Indicator/"No Video" Indicator: Shows when recording cannot take place normally.

4. External Recording Control: This allows the camera controls to be used to start/stop recording when the camera is connected via HDMI to a third-party recorder.

5. Timecode: Shows when timecode (with hour, minute, second, and number for each frame) are used when shooting videos (Menu > Video Recording Menu > Timecode).

6. Destination: Shows the memory card slot being used to record movies.

7. Picture Control: Shows current picture control (if set).

8. Available Recording Time: Shows the amount of time remaining until memory card will become full or maximum length of movie is reached.

9. Frame Size and Rate: Shows the current frame size and rate.

10. Hi-Res Zoom Indicator: Shows when Hi-res zoom is turned on.

11. Image Area: Shows the current image area: FX for full and DX for cropped area.

12. Video File Type: Shows selected video file type: NEV, MOV, and MP4 formats.

13. Recording Indicator: The border of the frame turns red when recording video.

14. Zoom Position for Hi-res zoom.

15. Sound Level: Shows the current sound levels. If red, then it's too high and the mic sensitivity needs to be reduced.

16. Audio Input Sensitivity: The sensitivity can be set for Auto or 1–20 (higher value is more sensitive).

17. Electronic VR Indicator: Shows if the Electronic Vibration Reduction feature is active.

MONITOR DISPLAY (MOVIE)

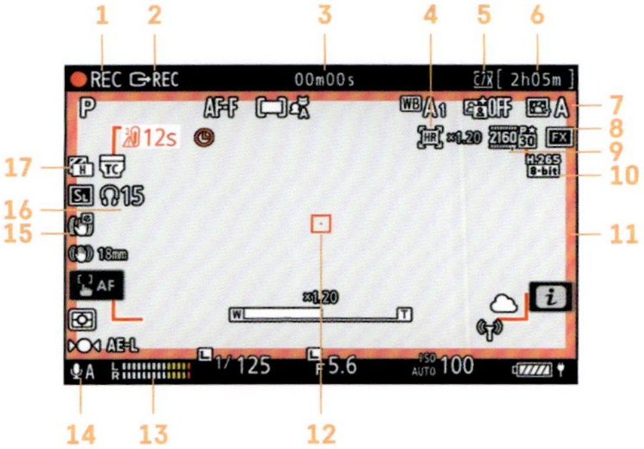

1. **Recording Indicator/"No Video" Indicator:** Shows when recording cannot take place normally.

2. **External Recording Control:** This allows the camera controls to be used to start/stop recording when the camera is connected via HDMI to a third-party recorder.

3. **Timecode:** Shows when timecode (with the hour, minute, second, and number for each frame) are used when shooting videos (Menu > Video Recording Menu > Timecode).

4. **Hi-Res Zoom Indicator:** Shows when Hi-res zoom is turned on.

5. **Destination:** Shows the memory card slot being used to record movies.

6. **Available Recording Time:** Shows the amount of time remaining until the memory card will become full or maximum length of movie is reached.

7. **Picture Control:** Shows current picture control (if set).

8. **Image Area:** Shows the current image area: FX for full and DX for cropped area.

9. **Frame Size and Rate:** Shows the current frame size and rate.

10. **Video File Type:** Shows selected video file type: NEV, MOV, and MP4 formats.

11. **Recording Indicator:** The border of the frame turns red when recording video.

12. **Zoom position** for Hi-res zoom.

13. **Sound Level:** Shows the current sound levels. If red, then it's too high and the mic sensitivity needs to be reduced.

14. **Audio Input Sensitivity:** The sensitivity can be set for Auto or 1–20 (higher value is more sensitive).

15. **Electronic VR Indicator:** Shows if the Electronic Vibration Reduction feature is active.

16. **Headphone Volume:** Shows the current headphone volume. Use the up and down keys on the Multi Selector to adjust the volume.

17. **Zebra Pattern:** When active, a zebra pattern is used to show tone range.

INFO DISPLAY

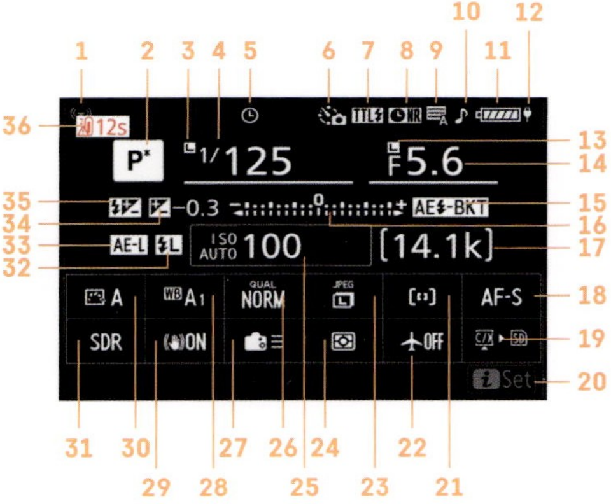

1. **Wi-Fi Connection:** Shows when there is an active Wi-Fi connect on.

2. **Shooting Mode:** Shows the current Shooting mode (Auto, P, S, A, M).

3. **Shutter Speed Lock Icon:** Shows when shutter speed is locked.

4. **Shutter Speed:** Shows the current shutter speed.

5. **Clock Icon:** Flashes when the camera time and date need to be reset.

6. **Interval-Timer Indicator:** Appears when using the interval-timer mode.

7. **Flash Control Mode:** Shows the current flash control mode.

8. **Long Exposure Noise Reduction Icon:** Shows when the long exposure noise reduction is active.

9. **Shutter Type:** Shows the type of shutter being used, either the mechanical shutter or the electronic front-curtain shutter. Or, set it to Auto, and the camera selects the shutter type.

10. **"Beep" Indicator:** Shows when the camera's beep is turned on for self-timer countdown, interval-timer photography, or focus confirmation (not in AF-C mode).

11. **Battery Indicator:** Displays the amount of power left in the battery.

12. **USB Power Delivery:** Shows when the camera is drawing power from a connected USB device.

13. **Aperture Lock Icon:** Shows when the current aperture is locked.

14. **Aperture:** Shows the current aperture.

15. **Exposure/Flash Bracketing Icon:** Shows when Exposure/Flash Bracketing is turned on.

16. **Exposure Indicator/Exposure Compensation:** Shows the current exposure value/Shows any exposure compensation adjustments.

17. **Number of Exposures Remaining:** Shows the number of remaining images that can be stored on the current memory card using the current image quality and image size settings.

18. **Focus Mode:** Shows the current Focus mode.

19. **View Memory Card Info:** Shows the card currently selected as the destination for new images and the options when both memory card slots are filled.

20. *i* **Icon:** Press Set to open the i Menu.

21. **AF-Area Mode:** Shows current AF-Area mode.

22. **Airplane Mode Status:** Shows whether or not airplane mode is activated.

23. **Image Size:** Shows the current image size.

24. **Metering Mode:** Shows the current Metering mode.

25. **ISO Value:** Shows the current ISO value.

26. **Image Quality:** Shows the current image quality.

27. **Custom Controls Icon:** Shows the custom operations performed in photo mode by the button, dials, and lens ring.

28. **White Balance:** Shows the current White Balance.

29. **Vibration Reduction Indicator:** Shows when the VR is active.

30. **Picture Control:** Shows current Picture Control setting.

31. **Tone Mode:** SDR for normal tone mode, and HLG for an extended tone range mode.

32. **Flash Value (FV) Lock Indicator:** Shows when the current flash value is locked.

33. **Autoexposure (AE) Lock Indicator:** Shows when the autoexposure value is locked.

34. **Exposure Compensation Indicator/Exposure Compensation Value:** Shows when exposure compensation is being applied/Shows the currently set exposure compensation value.

35. **Flash Compensation Indicator:** Shows when flash compensation is applied.

36. **Temperature Warning:** Shows when the camera sensor is getting too hot and needs to cool down.

CONTROL PANEL

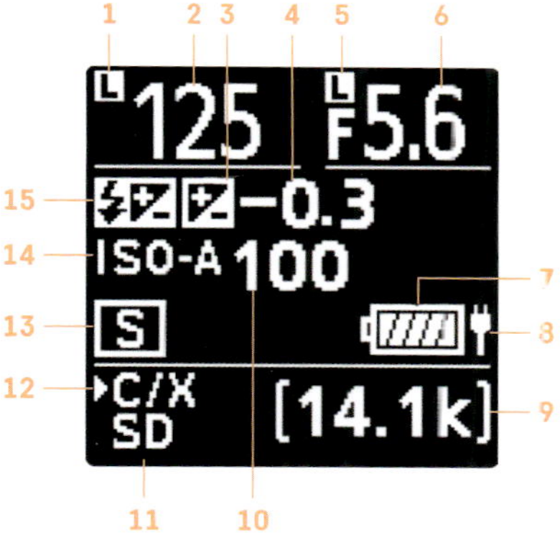

1. **Shutter Speed Lock:** Shows when shutter speed is locked.
2. **Shutter Speed:** Shows current shutter speed.
3. **Exposure Compensation Indicator:** Shows if exposure compensation is turned on.
4. **Exposure Compensation Value:** Shows how much the exposure will be adjusted.
5. **Aperture Lock:** Shows when aperture is locked.
6. **Aperture:** Shows current aperture value.
7. **Battery Indicator:** Shows battery life. Will flash when battery is dead and camera can no longer take photos.

8. **USB Power Delivery:** Shows when the camera is drawing power from a connected USB device.

9. **Number of Remaining Exposures:** Shows the number of remaining exposures.

10. **ISO:** Shows current ISO.

11. **Memory Card Indicator for SD card.**

12. **Memory Card Indicator for CFexpress/XQD card.**

13. **Release Mode:** Shows the current Release mode: S (Single Frame), L (Continuous Low), H (Continuous High), H* (Continuous High Extended). [C30] [C60] [C120]: camera takes 30, 60, or 120fps while shutter release is pressed. [Self-Timer] when in Self Timer mode.

14. **ISO Sensitivity Indicator:** Shows if Auto ISO is engaged.

15. **Flash Compensation Indicator:** Shows if any flash compensation is being used.

CONTROL PANEL (MOVIE)

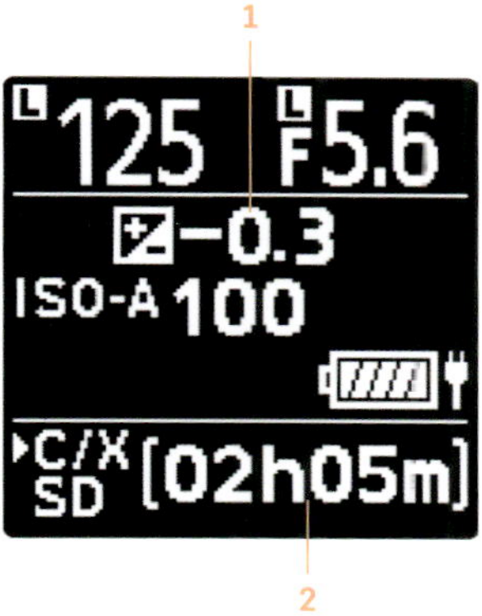

1. Exposure Compensation Value: Shows how much the exposure will be adjusted.

2. Available Recording Time: Shows the amount of time remaining until the memory card will become full or the maximum length of movie is reached.

03 ESSENTIAL MODES AND SETTINGS

MODE SHOOTING MODES

Press the Mode Dial Lock Release and rotate the Mode dial to choose the Shooting mode.

Auto (Auto): Point-and-shoot mode where the camera sets the exposure.

P (Programmed Auto): Camera sets shutter speed and aperture based on metering info and current ISO.

S (Shutter Priority): You set shutter speed, and camera sets aperture based on metering info and current ISO. Shutter speed can be set between 30 sec.–1/8000 sec. (1/2000 sec. when using electronic front-curtain shutter).

A (Aperture Priority): You set aperture, and camera sets shutter speed based on metering info and current ISO. Range of apertures depends on the lens.

M (Manual): You set both shutter speed and aperture. Can set shutter speed to Bulb mode for long exposures.

U1, U2, U3 (User Settings): You can assign frequently used settings to these three modes for quick recall.

METERING MODES

Press Menu > Photo Shooting Menu > Metering, or use the iMenu to set metering mode.

Matrix: Uses a wide area of the frame along with color, distance, tone distribution, and composition to determine exposure. Best for most situations.

Center-Weighted: Uses information predominantly from center of frame to determine exposure.

Spot: Uses area under current focus point to determine exposure.

Highlight-Weighted: Camera determines exposure to keep detail in the brightest highlights.

EXPOSURE COMPENSATION

Press Exposure Compensation button on top right of camera and turn Main Command dial to adjust exposure from −5 (darker) to +5 (lighter) in 1/3-stop increments in Photo mode, and −3 to + 3 in Movie mode.

Note: In Manual (M) exposure mode, Exposure Compensation will change exposure indicator but not shutter speed or aperture.

FOCUS MODES

Push Fn2 button and turn Main Command dial.

AF-S (Single AF): Focus starts when shutter release button is pressed halfway and locks when focus is achieved. Best for stationary subjects.

AF-C (Continuous AF): Focus starts when shutter release button is pressed halfway and continues to focus until photo is taken. Best for moving subjects.

AF-F (Full-Time AF): Available only in Movie mode. Focus tracks subject continuously until shutter release button is pressed halfway. Can really drain the battery.

M (Manual Focus): Focusing is accomplished by turning focusing ring on lens barrel.

AF-AREA MODES (FOCUS AREA)

Push Fn2 button and turn Sub-Command dial.

Pinpoint AF: For critical focus when AF-S (Single AF) Focus mode is used.

Single-Point AF: Uses single point for focus.

Dynamic-Area AF (S, M, L): User selects the focus point, and camera tries to keep moving subject in focus (AF-C only). The dynamic area can be selected from Small, Medium, or Large.

Wide-Area AF (S, L): Single wide point used for focusing. Small and large point sizes are available.

Wide-Area AF (C1, C2): Create and store custom AF-Area dimensions. The size options will depend on the image area selected.

3D Tracking: Tracks subject through the scene. Press and hold shutter release button halfway down to activate (AF-C only).

Subject Tracking AF: Tracks selected subject through the frame when shooting video. Press OK button or AF-ON button to activate. Press OK button to end tracking and refocus on the center of the frame.

Auto-Area AF: Camera focuses on the closest thing, but faces are given priority and the camera tries to focus on people over other objects.

RELEASE MODES

Press Release mode button and rotate Main Command dial.

S (Single Frame): Takes a single shot every time shutter release is pressed.

L (Continuous Low): Takes between 1–7 frames per second (FPS) as long as you press shutter release. Change the frame rate by pressing the Release mode button and rotate Sub-Command dial.

H (Continuous High): Takes up to 8.1 FPS (16 FPS when using electronic shutter) for as long as you press shutter release.

H* (Continuous High Extended): Takes up to 14 FPS (20 FPS when using electronic shutter) for as long as you press the shutter release.

(C30, C60, C120): The camera takes 30, 60, or 120 FPS. Only takes JPG/HEIF images and the number and speed will be impacted by memory card speeds.

Self-Timer: When shutter release is pressed fully, camera waits a set time before taking photo. To set the delay, press the Release mode button, and rotate the Sub-Command dial to choose the self-timer delay.

WHITE BALANCE

Press and hold the Fn1 button and rotate the Main Command dial.

The **A (Auto)** setting is best for most situations. White balance can be set to shift colors warmer, cooler, or keep them accurate. Other settings are all matched to different lighting types. For truest colors, pick the type of lighting being used to illuminate scene.

FILE FORMAT/IMAGE QUALITY

Menu > Photo Shooting Menu > Image Quality

RAW (NEF): The RAW data from the image sensor is recorded each time a photo is taken.

RAW (NEF) + JPEG/HEIF: The camera saves two files each time the shutter button is pressed: a RAW file and a JPEG (or HEIF) file. You can decide the quality of the JPEG/HEIF (fine, normal, or basic). Only the JPEG/HEIF is shown during playback. Deleting the JPEG also deletes the RAW file.

JPEG/HEIF: The camera saves a JPEG or HEIF file each time the shutter button is pressed. You can decide the quality of the JPEG/HEIF (fine, normal, or basic).

Note: When [SDR] is selected for [Tone mode] in the Photo Shooting Menu, the camera will record JPEG. When [HLG] is selected, the camera will record an HEIF File.

04 OTHER HELPFUL SETTINGS

PICTURE CONTROLS

Photo Shooting Menu > Set Picture Control

Eleven preset picture controls can all be adjusted: **A (Auto)**, **SD (Standard)**, **NL (Neutral)**, **VI (Vivid)**, **MC (Monochrome)**, **FM (Flat Monochrome)**, **DM (Deep Tone Monochrome)**, **PT (Portrait)**, **RP (Rich Tone Portrait)**, **LS (Landscape)**, **FL (Flat), C1-9 (Custom Picture Control)**, **[symbol]1-9 (Cloud Picture Control)**. You can modify the picture controls by adjusting Effect Level, Sharpness, Clarity, Contrast, Highlights, Shadows, Brightness, Saturation, Hue, Filter Effects, and Toning. Monochrome images can have a Yellow, Orange, Red, or Green filter applied.

FLASH MODES

Photo Shooting Menu > Flash Mode

Fill Flash: The flash fires with each shot. When using P or A shooting mode, camera uses shutter speeds between

1/60–1/200 sec. (1/60–1/8000 sec. when Auto FP High-Speed Sync is selected).

Red-Eye Reduction: Flash fires twice: first pre-flash burst is so that subject's pupils close, reducing the red-eye. Not good for moving subjects.

Slow Sync and Red-Eye Reduction: Combines red-eye reduction pre-flash and slow sync for better portraits taken when you want ambient light in photo. Available only in P and A shooting modes.

Slow Sync: Flash is used in conjunction with slower shutter speeds to allow ambient light into photo. Available only in P.

Rear-Curtain Sync: Flash fires at end of exposure, creating more natural-looking light trails if subject is moving.

Flash Off: Flash does not fire.

COLOR SPACE

Photo Shooting Menu > Color Space

sRGB: Smaller color space. Best when images are used directly from camera.

Adobe RGB: Larger color space. Best used when images will be edited with post-processing software.

HIGHLIGHT WARNING (BLINKIES)

Playback Menu > Playback Display Options, select Highlights

Shows pure white areas as blinking highlights on playback. Useful for determining if areas are being overexposed.

NOISE REDUCTION

Photo Shooting Menu > Long Exposure NR

Reduces noise in images with shutter speeds of 1 second or longer. Doubles time needed to save image to memory card.

Photo Shooting Menu > High ISO NR

Reduces noise in images taken at high ISO settings. Use Normal for default, Low for less noise reduction, and High for more noise reduction.

AUTO ISO

Hold ISO button and rotate Sub-Command dial to turn Auto ISO on or off.

You can set the **Maximum Sensitivity** (the highest ISO the camera will use) in Photo Shooting Menu > ISO Sensitivity Settings > Maximum Sensitivity.

DISP BUTTON

Press the DISP button to cycle through the available views on the monitor in Photo mode. Menu > Custom Setting Menu > Custom Monitor Shooting Display to set what screens are shown from the following choices:

Simple: View the shooting mode, shutter speed, aperture, and other basic shooting info.

Detail: View the focus mode, AF-area, white balance, and other detailed shooting information.

Touch Controls: View the options that can be accessed via touch controls, including touch AF and the i menu.

Virtual Horizon: Shows a virtual horizon, allowing you to adjust the camera until it is level. Useful for shooting landscapes.

Histogram: Shows a live histogram.

Framing Grid: Enable the framing grid.

Center Indicator: Shows crosshairs in the center of the frame.

Center-Weighted Area: Shows center-weighted area when center-weighted metering is being used.

Note: When in Movie mode, the Flash Info and Information Display options are not shown.

ACTIVE D-LIGHTING

Photo Shooting Menu > Active D-Lighting

Used to help preserve detail that can be lost in both the darkest and brightest parts of a high-contrast image. You can set the strength to Auto, Extra High, High, Normal, or Low, or you can turn Active D-Lighting off.

Note: This feature can cause image issues such as banding and noise at higher ISO settings.

BKT AUTO BRACKETING

Photo Shooting Menu > Auto Bracketing

Auto Bracketing is used to take a set of images where the exposure & flash, exposure, flash power, white balance, or Active D-Lighting is changed slightly between each frame. You can set the camera to whichever option you would like to bracket:

Exposure (AE) & Flash: Changes the exposure and the flash power.

Exposure (AE): Changes the exposure.

Flash: Changes the flash power.

WB: Changes the white balance.

ADL: Changes the amount of the Active D-Lighting applied.

You can also set the number of shots and the increment of change between each shot. For ADL bracketing, you adjust the Amount of change, not the Increment.

WIRELESS CONNECTION (SNAPBRIDGE)

Use the Nikon SnapBridge app on your smartphone or tablet to connect the Z6 III to the device.

Allows for wireless downloading of images and remote control of camera via Bluetooth. The Z6 III can also connect to a computer via the built-in Wi-Fi or to computers or FTP servers using the optional WT-7 wireless transmitter.

05 STEP-BY-STEP SHOOTING INSTRUCTIONS

MULTIPLE EXPOSURES

Create in-camera multiple exposures:

1. Select Photo Shooting Menu > Multiple Exposure, and press right on the Multi Selector.
2. Choose the Multiple Exposure mode:

   On (series): Takes multiple exposures until Off is selected.
   On (single): Takes one multiple exposure.
   Off: Turns multiple exposures off.
3. Select Number of Shots to combine (2 to 10 RAW files).
4. Pick the Overlay mode:

   Add: The images are combined without any modification.
   Average: Before the images are combined, the gain for each image is divided by the total number of images to create a proper exposure.
   Lighten: Camera uses only lightest pixels of each image to create an overall light image.
   Darken: Camera uses only darkest pixels of each image to create an overall dark image.

5. Choose whether to keep the individual images by selecting Keep All Exposures and choosing On or Off, then pressing OK.

6. Choose whether to view the progress in the display by selecting Overlay Shooting and choosing On or Off, then pressing OK.

Note: Multiple exposures shot with the RAW file type will be recorded as JPEG format.

HDR HDR

Combine two images to reduce the contrast and improve tonal range:

1. Select Photo Shooting Menu > HDR Overlay, and press right on the Multi Selector.

2. Choose to shoot either a single occurrence (On [single photo]) or a series (On [series]), which will continue to shoot HDR until you select Off in HDR mode.

3. Choose HDR Strength from: Auto, Extra High, High, Normal, or Low.

4. Choose whether to keep the individual exposures (Save Individual Raw Images).

5. Press the shutter release once to take photos.

TIME-LAPSE MOVIES

Create a time-lapse movie in-camera:

1. Select Photo Shooting Menu > Time-Lapse Movie, and press right on the Multi Selector.
2. Select the Interval: the time between each photo. Set in minutes and seconds.
3. Select the Shooting Time: how long to shoot (up to 23 hours and 59 minutes).
4. Choose whether you want to use Exposure Smoothing. When On, it automatically tries to smooth any big changes in the exposure.
5. Turn the Electronic Shutter On or Off.
6. Choose the Image Area to capture.
7. Choose Image Area (FX or DX).
8. Choose the Video file type (Mov or MP4).
9. Choose the Frame Size/Frame Rate for the final output.
10. Turn Interval Priority On or Off. On ensures that frames shot in P or A mode will use the set interval even if that creates an underexposed image.
11. Choose whether the camera focuses between shots: If turned on, the camera will try to focus before each new shot using the currently selected Focus mode.

12. Choose the destination: Pick which card slot to use when there are two memory cards in the camera.

13. Select Start and press OK.

INTVL INTERVAL TIMER PHOTOGRAPHY

Set the camera to take a series of photos over a period of time:

1. Select Photo Shooting Menu > Interval Timer Shooting, and press right on the Multi Selector.

2. Set Start options to begin now or at least 1 minute in the future (Choose Day/Time).

3. Set the Interval between photos (Hours/Minutes/Seconds).

4. Set number of intervals and the number of shots per interval (Intervals x Shots/Interval).

5. Turn Exposure Smoothing On or Off.

6. Turn Silent Photography On or Off.

7. Turn Interval Priority On or Off. When On, photos shot in P or A mode will be taken at the chosen interval; when Off, the photos will use shutter speed to achieve proper exposure even if that is longer than the selected interval.

8. Choose whether the camera focuses between shots: If turned on, the camera will try to focus before each new shot using the currently selected Focus mode.

9. Choose additional options: You can choose AE bracketing, and creating a Time-Lapse movie. If AE Bracketing is selected, choose the Number of Shots and Increment. If Time-Lapse movie is selected, choose the frame size, frame rate, and the memory card where the final movie will be saved.

10. Choose the starting folder for your images.

11. Highlight Start and press OK. If you selected Now as the starting time, the camera will begin taking images. If you set the start time for later, it will start at the specified time.

SHOOTING SCENARIO
PORTRAIT

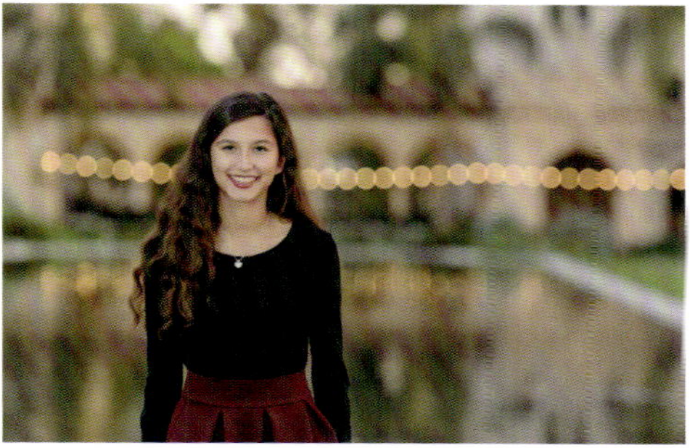

KEY PRINCIPLES

- The key to a portrait like this is shallow depth of field. So shoot in **APERTURE PRIORITY** mode and start with the lowest aperture your lens offers (such as **f/2.8 or f/4**).
- Remember to **focus on the eyes**.

- If the image is too dark or too light, use **EXPOSURE COMPENSATION** to adjust the brightness level.
- If the image is blurry from a slow shutter speed, **raise the ISO** to increase your sensor's sensitivity to light, thus allowing for a faster shutter speed.
- Remember to use a **focal length of 50mm or greater** so that you don't distort your subject's face.

SHOOTING SCENARIO
GROUP PORTRAIT

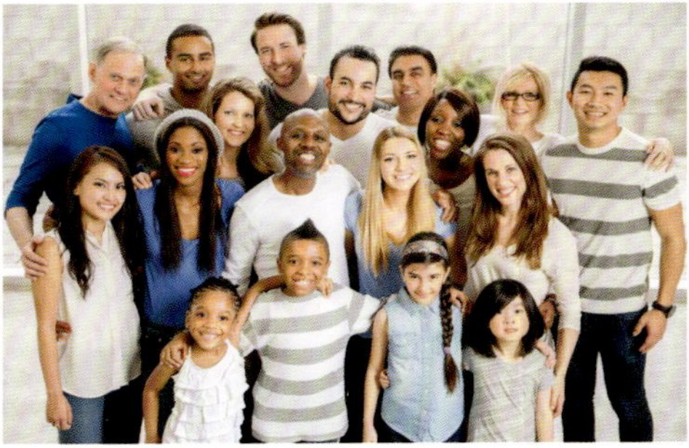

KEY PRINCIPLES

- In order to get everyone in focus, you need a deep depth of field. So shoot in **APERTURE PRIORITY** mode and set the aperture between **f/8–f/16**.
- **Focus on the person in the middle of the group.** Check focus by using the Zoom In button to view it at 100% and check faces in the front and back rows. If anyone is out of focus, use a smaller aperture for deeper depth of field.
- Use **MATRIX METERING** to account for the light in the entire scene.
- **Arrange the group so they can all see you** (and you can see them).
- Use **EXPOSURE COMPENSATION** if the image is too bright or too dark.
- If image is blurry, **raise the ISO** to allow the camera to use a faster shutter speed.

SHOOTING SCENARIO
LANDSCAPE

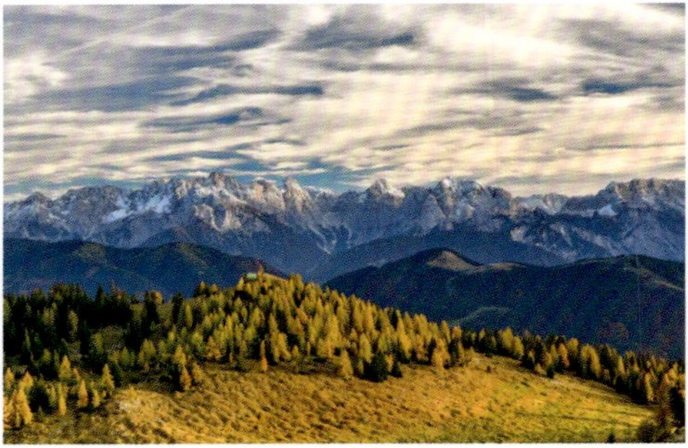

KEY PRINCIPLES

- Shoot in **APERTURE PRIORITY** to control depth of field, and start with **f/16** to ensure deep depth of field.
- **Use a tripod** to eliminate camera movement. Whenever your camera is on a tripod, also make sure that **VIBRATION REDUCTION is turned off**.
- Use **MATRIX METERING** mode and **SINGLE AUTOFOCUS (AF-S)** Focus mode.
- **Set the ISO to a low setting (100–200)** to avoid any digital noise.

- Shoot in **RAW** so that you have the most available information when editing later.
- Consider **BRACKETING** your exposures.

SHOOTING SCENARIO
FREEZE ACTION

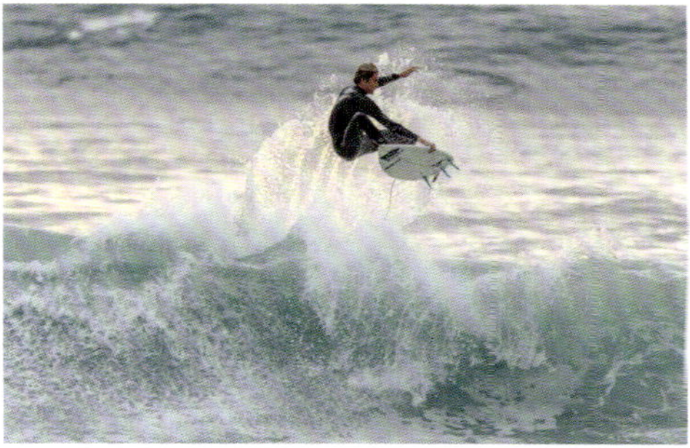

KEY PRINCIPLES

- Use **SHUTTER PRIORITY** mode and set the shutter speed to a value that will freeze the action. The appropriate shutter speed depends on your subject and its movement, but could be anywhere between **1/500–1/8000 sec**.

- Use **CONTINUOUS AUTOFOCUS (AF-C)** so that the camera keeps focusing as the subject moves.
- If the image is dark or blurry, **raise the ISO** or try AUTO ISO to automatically have the camera adjust the ISO as needed.

SHOOTING SCENARIO
SHOWING MOTION—PANNING

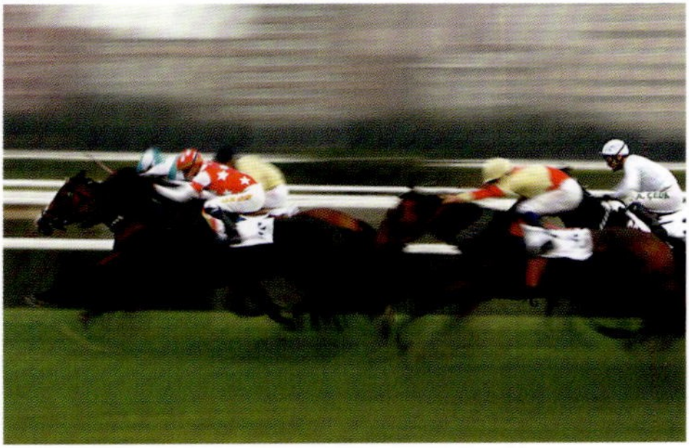

KEY PRINCIPLES

- Shoot in **SHUTTER PRIORITY** mode and use a slow-enough shutter speed to allow for the subject to move during the exposure.
- **Follow the subject** across the frame as you shoot.

- Try using **LIVE VIEW**, which allows you to see the subject during the exposure.
- Use **CONTINUOUS AUTOFOCUS (AF-C)**, as well as **DYNAMIC-AREA AF**.

SHOOTING SCENARIO
LOW-LIGHT ACTION

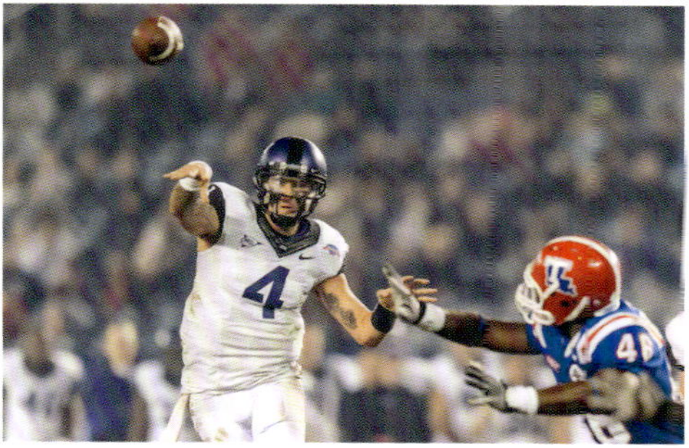

KEY PRINCIPLES

- Shoot in **APERTURE PRIORITY** mode and use a wide aperture such as **f/2.8 or f/4**.
- Use **SPOT METERING** and meter on the subject's face.
- Use **CONTINUOUS AUTOFOCUS (AF-C)** and a single AF point.

- **Set the ISO to 1600 or higher**, depending on the amount of available light.
- If the image is blurry, **increase the ISO** to allow for a faster shutter speed.

SHOOTING SCENARIO
LONG EXPOSURE

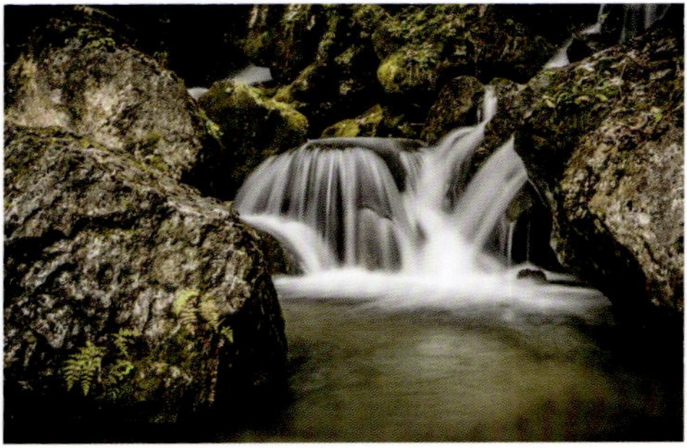

KEY PRINCIPLES

- Use **MANUAL** shooting mode, which allows you to use the **BULB** or **TIME** setting for long exposures.

- **Use a tripod** to keep the camera stable. **Turn off any VIBRATION REDUCTION feature**.
- Use the **SINGLE AUTOFOCUS (AF-S)** Focus mode, or try manual focus if the camera is having a hard time locking on focus.
- **Use a low ISO (100–400)** and **shoot RAW** to ensure a high-quality file.
- Use a **cable release** with a lock to avoid touching (shaking) the camera.

SHOOTING SCENARIO
MACRO/CLOSE-UP

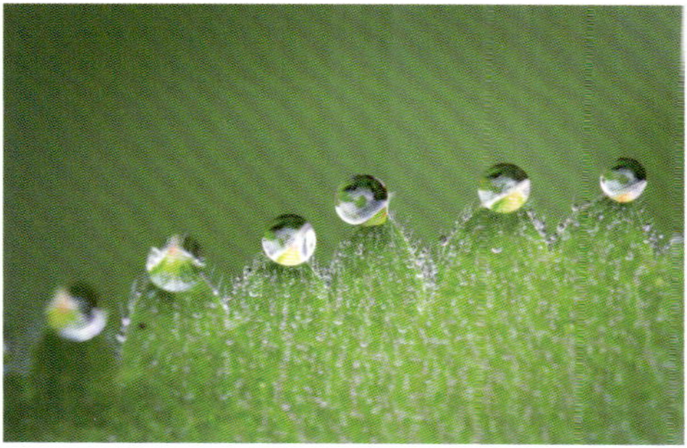

KEY PRINCIPLES

- Shoot in **APERTURE PRIORITY (Av)** mode and **use a small aperture** to ensure you achieve enough depth of field (this image was shot at f/13).
- Use **EVALUATIVE METERING** to analyze the light in the entire frame.
- A **tripod** is very useful for keeping the camera steady.
- Use **MANUAL FOCUS** and **zoom in** to confirm your focus is tack-sharp.
- Try using a dedicated **macro lens** or **close-up filters** to make sure you can achieve sharp focus when you're so close to the subject.

SHOOTING SCENARIO

VIDEO RECORDING/VLOGGING

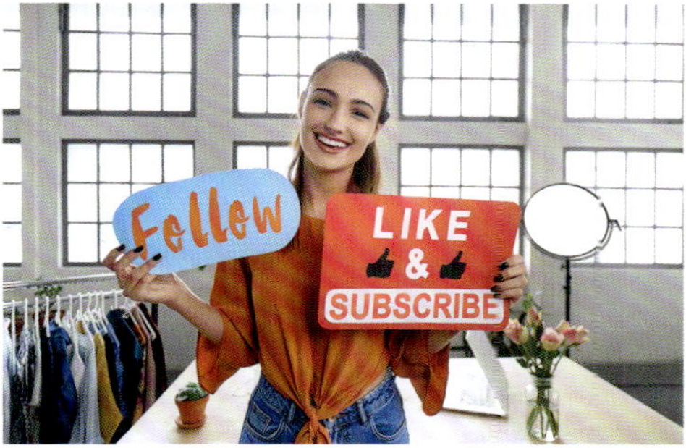

KEY PRINCIPLES

- Use a **shallow depth of field** to keep the viewers' attention on the subject. A **wide aperture** will keep the subject in focus while having the area in front of and behind the subject fall out of focus.
- Use **24 fps** for a more cinematic look.
- Set the **shutter speed** to **twice the frame rate**, or as close as you can get. If using 24 fps, the shutter speed should be 1/50 (or 1/60) second.

- Use an **external microphone** for better sound. The Rode VideoMic GO II is a great starter microphone.
- Keep the camera stable with a **tripod or gimble**. Smooth footage looks more professional.
- Use the **swing-out monitor** to watch the video being recorded. Remember to leave a second of two of nothing at the beginning and end of your video clips—this will make them much easier to edit later.